Editor's Heart

Praise the Lord and Welcome to another issue of Gospel 4 U Magazine.

As 2013 comes to a close I would like to remind some and encourage others that we have to "Finish Strong" We are not in this race to lose and we have to entrust that into our hearts that with God we are already winners, so begin to run this race with the attitude of a winner.

Usain Bolt is the fastest man alive and I know, without a shadow of a doubt the he does not go into any of his races thinking defeat, we as children of God have to step it up, we have to run the race set before us and know that we are already victorious.

Now in fact all who want to live godly lives in Christ Jesus will be persecuted. However, No weapon that is formed against us **WILL** prosper, we must continue in the things you have learned and are confident about. You know who taught you and before He formed you He knew you, so we can rest assured that God got us!!!!

He is able to give us wisdom, knowledge and understanding. Finish this year studying your WORD, Every scripture is inspired by God and useful for teaching, for reproof, for correction, and for training in righteousness, that the person dedicated to God may be capable and equipped for every good work. (2 Timothy 3:12-17)

"Don't give up, no matter how hard it gets. Run hard, finish strong."

God Bless!

Content

HOLIDAY RECIPES
8

KAREN ORLANDO
PAGE 4

PROPHET DANIEL PRINGLE
PAGE 11

KELLY CREWS
PAGE 22

** Editing by Stephanie Montgomery
** Contributions of Photos by Dr. Denise Jones

FINISH STRONG

Pastor Rebecca Cooper
8

Shopping on A Budget
12

Pastor Larry Birchett Jr
13

Dr. Tamika Wilson
18

Pastor Karen Orlando

Exclusive Interview By Prophetess Ayanna Moore

G4U: Thank you Pastor Karen Orlando for speaking with Gospel 4U Magazine. I was looking at your website and reading your testimony and WOW you don't have just one testimony, you have many.

Pastor Karen Orlando: Yes and many more to come, I tell you it never stops.

G4U: Amen! If you can, please share with our readers a little more about yourself. What are you currently doing? You are Pastoring a church, is that correct?

Pastor Karen Orlando: Yes we are Pastoring a Bible study and are currently looking for a building. We started about nine years ago with two people, but we have really grown. It's every Tuesday night and 1st and 3rd Sunday nights. God has been really awesome with it. People have been touched and growing. It is multicultural and God has been moving in the midst. I also travel around the country preaching and singing. I have three kids, I have a husband and I am pretty busy. God is just awesome!

G4U: I see that part of your testimony is that you were tone deaf, yet now the Lord is using you through song. Can you briefly explain?

Pastor Karen Orlando: I never wanted to sing. My dream was to be a professional dancer. I use to dance and was really good and people thought I had a future in it. Dancing was kind of the 'be all, end all' of my life. I did not think singing was an option because I was tone deaf - in fact, I also was born with a form of autism. Long story short, when I was thirteen years old I got saved and I said to the Lord, "Lord, I want to serve you. Here's my life do with it whatever you want." The first thing that He said was "Karen, I want you to give up dancing." At first I was so angry because I said, "Lord it is the only thing that I can do, it's the only thing that I have." It didn't make sense being a teenager coming to the Lord saying "Lord I will give you everything" and He is like "Ok give up your dancing". You kind of go back and forth arguing with Him. Finally, one day my mom comes out in the backyard and says, "Karen I have something to tell you that I don't think you are going to like very much." I said, "I know God wants me to give up dancing" and she said "Yeah, that's right." So a couple of weeks after this, I was in my bedroom and I began to pray and say "God I don't understand why you want me to give up dancing, it is the only thing in my life, but if that is what you want from me then I will do it." The Lord spoke to me and said "Karen I never take away without replacing it with something greater. Obedience is better than sacrifice." Then literally overnight, I was standing in my room and I just began to sing. My mother came upstairs and was banging on the door saying, "Turn the music off it's time to go to bed." I was like "Mom it's not music it's me!"

G4U: Wow!

Pastor Karen Orlando: Yes it was like God broke all the rules. Most people get hands laid on them and an impartation from somewhere, but this was just between me and God. Around the same time that the Lord blessed me to be able to sing, my father was getting ready to graduate from Bible school and as people were graduating and starting their churches, they would need someone to come and sing - so God just started opening up doors. Before I knew it I was 13-14 years old in full-time ministry.

G4U: That is amazing but it came after an amazing sacrifice. Even at the age you were, you were still willing to put up a big sacrifice.

Pastor Karen Orlando: One thing the Lord has taught me is that everything comes down to obedience - obedience and sacrifice. Sacrifice is when you give what you would rather keep for yourself. God is always looking to give you more than what you ever had. So when God is asking you for something, He is not asking you because He wants to rob you of something or to make you have less. When you can give him what is precious to you and put it in His hands, He multiplies it. It wasn't like I couldn't have touched lives or that God couldn't have used my dance to serve Him: but when He gave me the voice and the testimony, He took those talents and He multiplied. He gave me something inside of me that I never knew could exist. So sometimes when people are like "Oh I don't want to give this up. I don't want to sacrifice this" - they really miss the opportunity because God will always inconvenience you by taking you out of something you want to do, to put you in something that He has called you to do. When you are doing something that He has called, ordained, appointed and anointed you to do, you can walk in an authority and a freedom and go so much further than what you could have ever done yourself.

G4U: I believe I read that you and your husband were both on the worship team at your former church?

Pastor Karen Orlando: Yes, he sings and he stands by my side. He travels with me when I go out to minister. He sings backup for me when we are doing worship. He has been not only my greatest supporter and cheerleader, but the man of God that God has blessed me with to be able to walk through this life. He has enabled me and empowered me to do what I do.

G4U: How old are your children?

Pastor Karen Orlando: My oldest daughter is 18 and she just started college. My son is a junior and he is 16 years old. My youngest daughter is 14 and a freshman in high school. We are busy and they keep it real.

G4U: As I was reading through your bio it seems like you have been through a lot of tragedies, but also through a lot of triumphs. Do you believe all that you have been through is what helped you develop your relationship with God?

Pastor Karen Orlando: Absolutely! Absolutely! I was very very close to my dad. My dad was like the 'be all and end all' of my life. He was not just my dad, but because I was on the road traveling and ministering so much - I was not in church regularly, so he was also my Pastor. He was my manager. He did everything for me. It was difficult when he passed away because I was brought up that family was everything. In 1989 when my brother was tragically killed in a motorcycle accident - that was kind of the beginning of tragedies and from that point, it was like miracle after miracle after miracle. You know when you are living on the mountaintop and all of a sudden life happens, you feel like Wow I got the rug pulled out from under me. When my brother died, you can imagine. I don't think there is any greater pain than when a parent loses a child. What was so difficult for me was watching my mom and dad - who were the picture of stability, be devastated. Three short years later my father passed away. He died six months before I got married. A month before I got married, my mother was hit by a car and she almost died. When you go through so much tragedy at one time, sometimes Christians don't know what to say. They are often afraid of saying the wrong things, so they tend to not say anything and people start to withdraw. It just seemed like everything in my life died. I was newly married, but it was a very dark time. When my dad died, ministry stopped because it was my dad that was responsible for connecting me to people and my bookings. When he died no one was calling me anymore. There was so much that I did not know how to do for myself. I thought 'God you gave me all of this and now you have taken it all away.' Was it just for a season and now that season is over? But He who has begun a work is faithful to complete it.

G4U: So how did your singing career and ministry resurrect?

Pastor Karen Orlando: I had two kids in diapers at the time and my husband was not making a lot of money. We were finally in a local church, serving on the worship team. I was praying one night and God spoke to me and said, "It is time. I am going to get ready to send you out and I want you to do a record." At that point I said "God how am I going to do this? I don't have any money!" He said," I need you to step out on faith and to believe." Long story short, He brought the finances and I was able to lease the tracks and go into the studio. I was so afraid to go into the studio because I had never done anything without my dad. I said "God how can I do this without my father?" I will never forget the Lord saying, "Who gave you the father that you had? I did. I gave you that father to raise you but don't you ever forget you are my child." It was through losing my earthly father that propelled me into a place where I had to find out who my Heavenly Father was. Mountaintop experiences don't teach you anything. It is those valley experiences. What the enemy meant to destroy me with, God made me with.

G4U: Were there any moments where you can recall the Lord giving you supernatural strength to keep going?

Pastor Karen Orlando: I will never forget. I was going through something in my life and I was like "God where are you. I don't think that I am strong enough to handle this." I looked over at an afghan someone had made for the baby and God said "I want you to try to pull it apart." No matter how I pulled or stretched, it kept coming back together. God said, "That is how I made you, you are fearfully and wonderfully made. This blanket looks so pretty, elegant and dainty like you can just rip it apart, but I built you not to break. I built you to endure. I built you to go through the test." That's why Proverbs 3:5 says - trust in the Lord with all of your heart and lean not unto your own understanding. Sometimes you can't make sense of stuff. The first thing we have to stop doing is asking why. We may never know why, but it is the 'What'. The 'what' is what comes out of your tragedies. It is what God is building in you. You can either have negative faith or positive faith. Negative faith is; it will never happen. I can't do it. I don't have enough money. I am not the right weight. Or, you can have positive faith that says I CAN do all things through Christ who strengthens me. Nothing is too hard for God. Nothing is impossible. I thank God for the foundation I received in church growing up, but no one taught me about the process. Process is what happens when you pray and you sow and God says, "No, I am not doing it your way." When my brother and father died I was more shocked that God did not heal them, than I would have been if He had healed them. That is the kind of faith that I had. But if God always gave us everything we wanted - how would we learn to trust Him? Sometimes God will show us the end; that happy place, that promised land. But He is very smart - He doesn't show you the whole process and journey that will get you there because if you knew what you were going to go through, most of us would probably say "Uh, no thank you… I will stay where I am right now!" God is not just bringing us to a higher level - He is bringing us to new dimensions.

To read more of this interview with Pastor Karen Orlando, please go to http://issuu.com/home/publications and read our digital magazine!

Pastor/Prophetess Ayanna Moore
Empowerment Life Changing Temple
www.the-station.com

Finish Strong

When I think of a strong finish, I think of Jesus and His memorable last words, "It is finished". The work the Father had given Him on earth in His flesh was complete. Not only meaning the work He was sent to accomplish on the earth had come to an end – but that it was complete and fulfilled as well. That alone is encouraging to me: to know that everything I need or will ever need, has been provided through the finished work of Calvary.

Webster defines the word 'finish' as this; To complete or perfect. The word of God says in Psalms 138:8,

The LORD will perfect that which concerneth me: thy mercy, O LORD, endureth forever: not the works of thine own hands.

Meaning, just like His work of redemption - everything that concerns me, He will complete. Take a moment and think about that. How would this change the way you look at what you may be experiencing right now? If we really believed the Lord was completing and perfecting that which concerns us, we would worry less and praise more. The life of Jesus was complete, just as the life of a seed is complete when it has gone through all the cycles of its life germination - budding, blossoming and forming fruit. No matter what stage you may find your life in right now, you must remember Jesus is the author and finisher of your faith. It begins with Him and will certainly be completed by Him.

In the life of a believer, it is often at the moments when we 'appear' or feel the weakest, that we are really the strongest. HIS STRENGTH is made perfect through our weaknesses. Those times give God and His glory the opportunity to be seen in and through us and our circumstances. Could Jesus have shown Himself mighty and strong before and during His death? Certainly - He told Peter, "Do you think I could not pray to my Father and He give me more than twelve legions of angels?"

Our weaknesses are a constant reminder of our need of God. The Apostle Paul counted it a blessing to be afflicted. It is through our frailty His power is manifested. It is through your toughest seasons you will experience His greatest favor. He not only wants you to know Him as your deliverer, but your sustainer. Do not look upon your insufficiency to determine the outcome of this trial, but consider what the Lord told the Apostle Paul in 2 Corinthians 12:9-10 - "My grace is sufficient for thee for my strength is made perfect in your weakness"; and let us have the same response as the Apostle Paul, "most gladly therefore will I rather glory in my infirmities, that the power of Christ may rest upon me. Therefore I take pleasure in infirmities, in reproaches, in necessities, in persecutions, in distresses for Christ's sake: for when I am weak, then am I strong." You see, Paul knew that the favor of God was more valuable than what it had cost him. If not for the night, we would never get to experience nor appreciate the beauty of shining stars. To really finish strong we must focus more on HIS power and less on our weaknesses. Are you experiencing a setback, failure, disappointment or time of weakness? This is a perfect opportunity for the power of Christ to rest upon you! So how exactly do you finish strong? By accepting the finished work of the cross and allowing His strength to be perfected in your weakness. YOU too can FINISH STRONG!

By Pastor Rebecca Cooper

University of Phoenix, Class of 2013
The LORD makes firm the steps of the one who delights in him ~ Psalm 37:23

Thank you Lord for ALL your BLESSINGS on me, I would not have made it without you

Commencement Ceremony Fall 2013
Saturday, October 12, 2013, 2pm
Hershey Theatre 15 E. Caracas Ave, Hershey, PA 17033
Limited seating — please arrive early.

University of Phoenix

Recipe for The Holiday Season By Cala Allison

Candied Pineapple Sweet Potatoes

Ingredients
2 lbs sweet
1 cup dark brown sugar (more or less to taste)
1 16oz can pineapple chunks in juice
1tsp cinnamion
1tsp nutmeg
1tbsp vanilla extract
1 stick butter
Pinch of salt

Directions
Preheat oven to 400F
Cut sweet potatoes into 1 inch pieces and boil until half-tender. Drain and place in baking dish.
Drain pineapple juice (reserve the juice). Add Melt butter in medium saucepan. Add pineapple juice, sugar, cinnamon, nutmeg and vanilla extract. Add a pinch of salt. Cook over medium heat until the ingredients are incorporated. Reduce until semi-thickened.

*Sugar, cinnamon, nutmeg and vanilla amounts can be adjusted for taste.
Pour sauce over the pineapples and sweet potatoes.
Bake covered for approximately 20 minutes until potatoes are fully cooked. If the potatoes are already fully cooked, do not cover. Bake uncovered for an additional 10 minutes or until browned. Sprinkle with additional brown sugar at the end.

Cornbread Stuffing

Ingredients
8 Cups Cornbread (cubed)
6 tbsp of butter
1 cup celery, chopped
1 large onion, chopped
5 cups chicken stock
1 teaspoon salt
Freshly ground black pepper
1 tablespoon poultry seasoning (optional)
3 eggs, beaten
½ cup dried, sweetened cranberries (optional)

Directions
Preheat oven to 375 degrees F.
Place the cubed cornbread in a large bowl. Melt the butter in a large pan over medium heat. Add the vegetables and sauté until transparent. Set aside to cool for a few minutes and then add to cornbread. Whisk the eggs, chicken stock and seasonings together. Pour the egg mixture into the cornbread. Add the dried cranberries (optional). Combine all items and pour mixture into a greased pan. Cook covered for approximately 30 minutes. Uncover and cook for an additional 10-15 minutes until crusty.

For more recipes and feedback email us at
info@gospel4u.tv

Finishing Strong

By Prophet Daniel Pringle

We are moving down the home stretch of the year 2013. I believe that God wants to release a momentum into your life now that will thrust you into 2014 with a spirit of acceleration. Let me share some principles with you on the importance of finishing strong.

Psalm 65:11 - Thou crownest the year with thy goodness; and thy paths drop fatness.

A year constitutes a revolution of time. A year is a cycle. When you come to the end of a year you are coming to the end of revolution of time, the end of a cycle. How you end the year will determine how you start the next year. God does this by crowning the end of this year with goodness.

The word for goodness in Hebrew means "good, favor and increase". God wants you to end your year on a positive note with favor and increase. He then states 'that your paths will drop with fatness'. Fatness speaks of overflow, excess and abundance. The end of your year should be a time of abundance and overflow. This means that each month things in your life ought to be increasing to the degree that when you finish the year, you will leave evidence of success throughout each and every month. When your year is finished in this manner, you will experience accelerated momentum that will catapult you into your new cycle of success.

This is not automatic - but it is intentional. We must do things to cooperate in order for that to occur. Let me share some principles with you:

REVISIT YOUR VISION AND GOALS

What primary goal do you have - that if completed, would drastically improve your life or bring you fulfillment? This needs to be written and then read on a daily basis. This keeps you focused and intentional in life.

MAKE FAITH CONFESSIONS

You also need to get heaven's involvement. You do this by making faith confessions from the Word of God.

Mark 11:23-24 " Whosoever shall say unto this mountain, Be thou removed, and be thou cast into the sea; and shall not doubt in his heart, but shall believe that those things which he saith shall come to pass; he shall have whatsoever he saith". Therefore I say unto you, What things soever ye desire, when you pray, believe that you receive them, and ye shall have them."

BE ACTION-ORIENTED

What is the first thing that you can do - that once completed, will move you toward your goal? This may be a simple phone call, or putting in an application.

CELEBRATE VICTORIES

Every winning season begins with small victories. Learn to be a person of thanksgiving. Giving thanks is one of the most powerful tools in the hands of a believer.

God desires for your year to be crowned with goodness so that you will finish the year strong with abundance and increase in every area of your life.

SHOPPING ON A BELIEVABLE BUDGET

To reach the contributors Jennifer Marlowe and Odinae Fisher, a Mother and Daughter team contact

Jennifer Marlowe @

auntypministries@gmail.com

And Odinae Amoi Fisher @

Nothingtowear2@gmail.com

http://nothingtoweartoo.blogspot.com/

(Above) Dress: Free people $68
Shoes: Nordstrom $88

(Below) Dress: Macys $28
Cardigan: Marshalls $19
Accessories: Charming

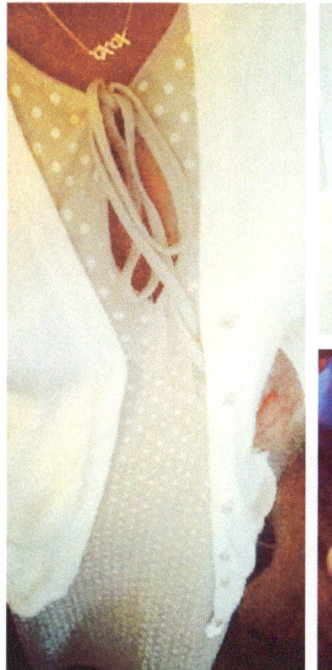

Shopping is never a hard job, but staying within budget can sometimes be a challenge. And not being open minded and trusting your sense of style can take the fun out of shopping. You can have a fabulous wardrobe on a Believable Budget. People maybe shock by how fabulous you look and how little you paid for it, but there are easy ways to look beautiful without breaking the bank.

When shopping for Name Brands for less, it's a good idea to wait on the department stores double coupons days like friends and family day. You end up getting up to 40-70% off sale at Lord &Taylor!

We value your feedback.

Jennifer Marlowe & Odinae Fisher

Overcoming Storms

Pastor Larry Birchett Jr

There are times in our lives when God will take us from one realm of faith to another. He uses many vehicles to transport us such as: persecutions, trials, tribulations, pain, and even situations that I call storms. However we should understand that there is always purpose in our pain. We should know that there are multiplicities of fiery trials, but thank God that for every trial there is a faith that enables us. This faith is the vehicle that God will use to allow you to overcome every storm in your life.

Understand that your storm wasn't sent to kill you or even destroy you. It was sent to displace you. It was sent to displace you beloved because storms always displace things. God blesses us in places not time because He's not regulated by time. He lives in eternity and steps into time to "see" about us. To raise up a standard against the enemy, to fight our battles, to lead us into our purpose and to fulfill His promise concerning us.

In order to receive this revelation you have to understand the power of place. Places matter dear one. Therefore be cognizant of your "place." Fighting from the wrong place can be fatal. Are you wondering why it seems your prayers are not being answered? You're fighting from the wrong place. Fight from the Heavens my brothers and sisters because you're in a spiritual war. The Bibles says that we wrestle not against flesh and blood but against principalities, powers, ruler of the darkness of this age, against spiritual hosts of wickedness in the "heavenly" places…refer to Ephesians 6:12.

Fight from the Heavens because the battle is being waged in the Heavens. Fight in the spiritual because your battles are won in that realm or place. God told Joshua in **Deuteronomy 3:22** *you must not fear them, for the Lord your God Himself fights for you.*

In **Revelations 12:7-8** it says *And war broke out in Heaven and Michael and his angels fought with dragon; and the dragon and his angels fought but 8) but they did not prevail, nor was a "place" found for them in Heaven any longer.*

These scriptures and many more clearly identify where the real warfare is being waged. It is being waged in the spiritual realm and we have to know how to conduct warfare *there*. Lucifer and His angels were kicked out of the "place" of Third Heavens and he and his angels now continually conduct warfare against us in the Second Heavens. God is constantly sending angels to fight for you beloved and He's waiting for you to give permission for Him to send more. God does not exist in the flesh, Therefore He doesn't warfare in the flesh. He is Spirit and those who worship Him must worship Him in Spirit and Truth. Just like we worship Him with our mouths we conduct warfare with our mouths. Which is why I always say that the most powerful amongst us are those that pray without ceasing and have an excellent relationship with God.

Notice verse 11-12 of the book of Revelations because they encapsulate the point of this article: *11.) And they overcame him by the blood of the Lamb and by the <u>word of their testimony</u> and they did not love their lives to death. 12.) Therefore rejoice O heavens, and you who dwell in them! Woe to the inhabitants of the earth and sea! For the devil has come down to you, having great wrath, because he knows that he has a short time."*

We overcome by the word of our testimony beloved. God sent you into the test to deliver you with a testimony. He will turn the mess in your life into a message. He will use your storms to give you a strength that can never be taken away from you. In the end you will overcome if you don't give up. Go through the storm because if God brought you to it, it's His responsibility to bring you through it. You are more than conquerors beloved and in the end you will be better for have going through your storm

Breaking the Barriers of Adversity ~ 5 Key Elements

Coffee in hand, computer in lap and several deadlines to meet, I silently ask myself "what to write?" So many would look at a situation like this and identify it as the "spirit of procrastination", I on the other hand, view this setting as a beautiful opportunity to finish strong. It's kind of like admiring a difficult situation with the mindset of making lemonade with lemons.

By Tennie Alexander

A countless amount of great leaders have said this before and I will say it is as well, "Everything begins in the mind." Whether it's to start and finish something or simply persevere, our thoughts have the potential to be the battleground to conqueror outrageous wars or the playground for "ring around the defeat".

Nonetheless, God has given us the power to choose. Luke 10:19 tells us *"I have given you authority to trample on snakes and scorpions and to overcome all the power of the enemy; nothing will harm you."* (NIV) The proof is in our instruction manual that we are never without equipment; therefore, thankfully we can choose to win.

Bear in mind, however, with every decision to win will come that one uninvited guest; adversity. 1 Peter 4:12-13 *"12 Dear friends, do not be surprised at the fiery ordeal that has come on you to test you, as though something strange were happening to you. 13 But rejoice inasmuch as you participate in the sufferings of Christ, so that you may be overjoyed when his glory is revealed."*

Despite the expected mishaps that are sure to come, thankfully we have been provided with the proper equipment to win. Here are 5 points we should put to use in finishing strong and overcoming adversity using the Word of God:

1) Think

2) Declare

3) Apply

4) Overcome

5) Press

*Put your mind in alignment with the goal at hand. **Think** it to completion. (or for as he thinks within himself, so he is) Philippians 4:8 *"Finally, brothers, whatever is true, whatever is honorable, whatever is just, whatever is pure, whatever is lovely, whatever is commendable, if there is any excellence, if there is anything worthy of praise, think about these things."*

*Once you have the goal in your mind. Speak life to it vocally by declaring what you will fulfill

Job 22:28 *""You will also decree a thing, and it will be established for you; And light will shine on your ways."*

*When working to complete a God-ordained goal you will be faced with doubt, laziness and all sorts of obstacles, therefore there will be a time to prevail. We overcome with the Word of God, by prayer and by doing what is necessary not what we necessarily want to do. Beat all odds by executing despite all barriers.

Galatians 5:16-17 "So I say, live by the Spirit, and you will not gratify the desires of the sinful nature. For the sinful nature desires what is contrary to the Spirit, and the Spirit what is contrary to the sinful nature. They are in conflict with each other, so that you do not do what you want."

*In the end it will be the pressing that results in success. Press past the negative thoughts and any other obstacles by walking in the spirit. We walk in the Spirit by reading, praying, fasting and all else will fall in place.

2 Corinthians 12:9-10 " But he said to me, "My grace is sufficient for you, for my power is made perfect in weakness."Therefore I will boast all the more gladly about my weaknesses, so that Christ's power may rest on me. That is why, for Christ's sake, I delight in weaknesses, in insults, in hardships, in persecutions, in difficulties. For when I am weak, then I am strong.."

Finally as we remember the Word of God is used for teaching, rebuking, correcting and training in righteousness (2 Timothy 3:16-17), we can then assuredly apply it in everything we do and therefore finish strong, breaking through the barriers of adversity.

5 Keys to Finishing Strong In Your Marriage

The Real Love Show with Patricia Benjamin

'Together they go off hand-in-hand, rapturously in love' - and of course they live happily ever after!

Unfortunately real life bears little relation to the beautiful Hollywood movies. It looks nothing like what we read in romance novels. If so, the divorce rate inside and outside the church would not be so high. What do we do to ensure we not only start out strong and full of love, but that we finish strong too?

I was told when I set out on the road of marriage nearly 30 years ago that as we were both believers, it was going to be perfect and that Christ was our foundation- and all we needed to do was pray. Well, if only things had been that easy. While marriage is sacred and honourable, it is not all spiritual.

In fact some things feel very basic and routine. It's not exciting all the time. Sometimes the children are hard work. Sometimes keeping the home spic and span is hard work. Sometimes just being romantic is hard work. But all the hard work is worthwhile. Marriage is beautiful and amazing. Anything good doesn't come easy or cheap.

1. Love is about commitment. Not feelings. Not sex. Not aesthetics.

2. Love is work. Love is a verb. A doing word. Show your love by action and attitude.

3. Love is kind. Treat your partner with gentle understanding. Try a little tenderness.

4. Love is respect. Do nothing that dishonours them, but always show regard and esteem.

5. Love is fun. Keep things light. Remember to laugh. Don't take everything so seriously. A cheerful heart is like good medicine.

Keeping all 5 keys active in your marriage will keep love alive and ensure you finish strong!

Check out her radio show at www.ruachradio.com
My show is the RealLoveShow
Broadcasts Monday 2pm EST/ 11am PST/1pm CST

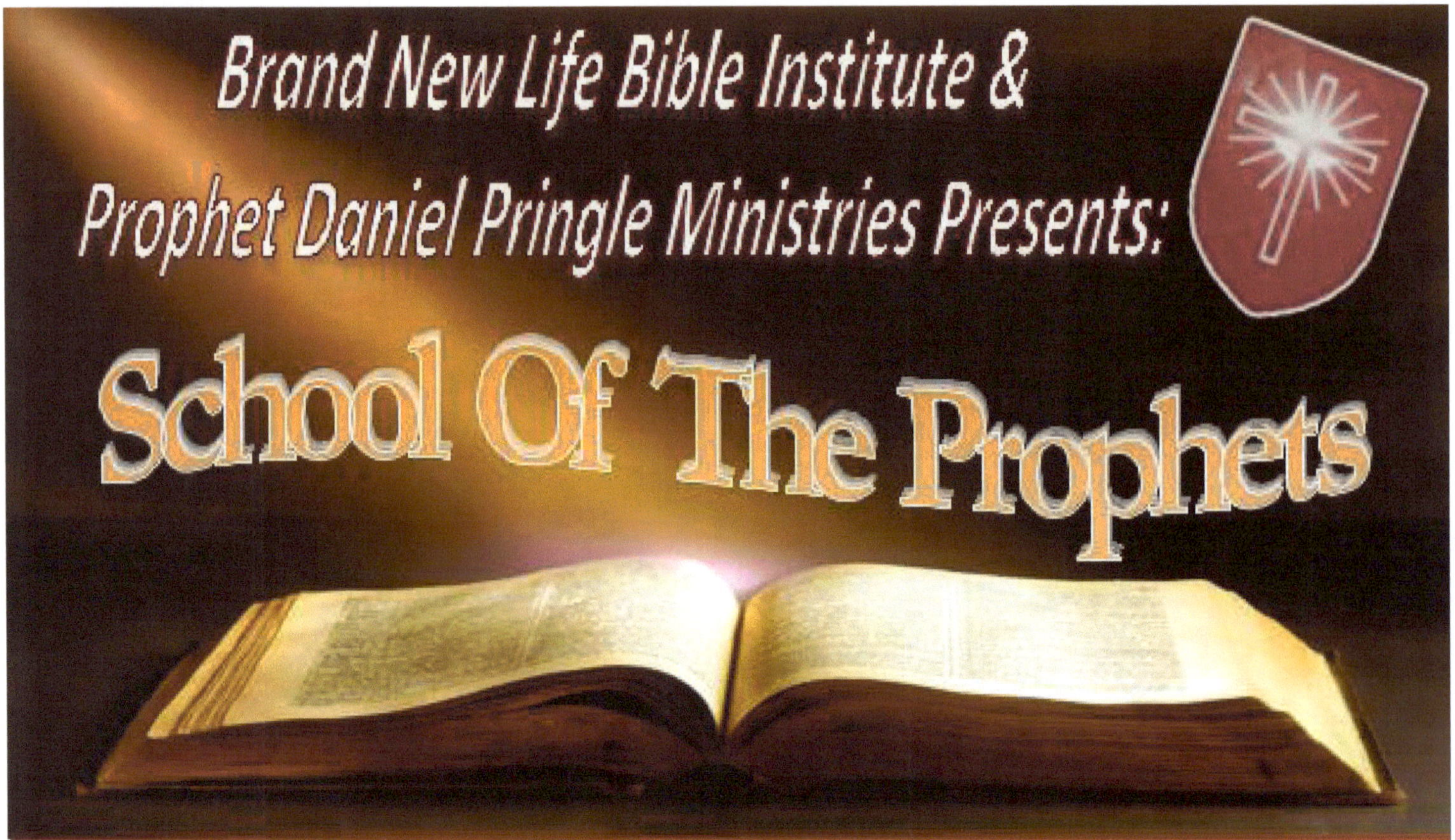

Brand New Life Bible Institute & Prophet Daniel Pringle Ministries Presents:

School Of The Prophets

School Of The Prophets

Begins Fri., Jan 3rd 2014 @ 7pm and Sat., Jan 4th 2014 @ 10am
Two classes per month will be offered (Fri & Sat) for four (4) months
Certificate awarded upon successful completion. (8 classes total)
There is a registration fee of $20 per semester. Classes are $25 each
Classes can be paid in monthly installments of $50/month or paid in full
$200 for the full semester. ($220 total w/registration fee)
You can register online and pay via PayPal on our website:
BNLCConline.org

Classes will be held at:
Brand New Life Christian Center
6301 Germantown Ave., Philadelphia, PA 19144
215.844.0790   bnlcc6301@verizon.net
Apostle Earl & Rev. Maria Palmer
Founders & Pastors

DANIEL PRINGLE
dpm
MINISTRIES
www.danielpringle.com

Finishing Strong

by Dr. Tamika Wilson

In keeping with the theme of "Finishing Strong", I would like to share this wise counsel and foreknowledge from the Lord. Not only is it for me, it is also for you.

The Lord spoke very clearly to me and said, *"During this upcoming Fall season it will be a time to store up, because some things and people are going to fall away. Just like the leaves fall from the trees, so will some things fall from your life."* He said it is a time to store up Spiritually (get more into His Word), Physically (rested, stop moving so much), Emotionally (don't get so caught up with things and people), Financially (to start saving, cut spending habits, to revisit my budget) and Socially (lose old connections and make new ones). He said it is imperative to store up because when we embrace the Winter season, it will be a rough season for some people. The Winter season is a hard season - this year it will be harder than before. That which we store up will carry us through the Winter season. I pondered on that Word and it lay heavy on my spirit. I prayed and asked the Lord: What is it? Who is it? Why? In this season we are now in, it is crucial to be obedient to this Word.

> **"Prophetically, the Fall season is a season of New things - it is also a season of harvest."**

Prophetically, the Fall season is a season of New things - it is also a season of harvest. The scriptures declare in Isaiah [18]- Remember ye not the former things, neither consider the things of old. [19] Behold, I will do a new thing; now it shall spring forth; shall ye not know it? Jer 5:24 - Neither say they in their heart, Let us now fear the LORD our God, that giveth rain, both the former and the latter, in his **season**: he reserveth unto us the appointed weeks of the harvest. Lastly, Ecc 3:1 - To everything there is a **season**, and a time to every purpose under the heaven: Pro 6:8 [6] - Go to the ant, thou sluggard; consider her ways, and be wise:....[8] Provideth her meat in the summer, and gathereth her food in the harvest......[11] So shall thy poverty come as one that travelleth, and thy want as an armed man.

It is time to release all toxic relationships, we are too busy and move around too much and most of us don't spend time in His presence asking Him, instead of others for direction. We don't meditate on His Word - we borrow when He has given the power of wealth into our hands (Deu 8:18). This is also a season of Harvest. That seed that you have sown, it is time to reap. Go back after it and declare: "Father, at your Word you said" It is also defined as the gathering of things planted - a natural time of reaping in joy what has been produced during the year in an agricultural community.

With the government shutdown occurring - God starting manifesting His Word. The Global Economy is in disarray. Federal programs are in jeopardy of losing their finances, pay checks have stopped, shop-lifting and crime are rising. This is only a sign of what the Lord is doing. People are turning away from God when they should be running to Him. These are the times we need Him the most. This is a time to pray and seek the Lord while He is near. This is not the time to be distressed nor depressed, but Joyful because of the plans He has for you. Psalm 30:5 - Weeping may endure for a night (season) but JOY. Your joy is on the horizon. I beseech you my readers, take heed to the Word of the Lord. Some of us the Lord has impregnated: this is not the time to abort your assignment - carry the weight, it is only resting upon you now weighing you down. You will give birth to what the Lord has promised.

You WILL reap if you faint not. There are people who are close to you that you will have to cut off and the Lord is showing them to you now. God is saying, *"Rest yourself, rest your spirit, feed off of me. Believe in me, and stop being so emotionally driven."* Once you get through this season I guarantee you, those unexpected bills that will come in the Winter season - God will see to it that they are paid. Those things that will be bitter and cold - God will bring peace and comfort. God does not change because of our circumstances - He is sending His Word to change our circumstances. Store Up. in me, and stop being so emotionally driven." Once you get through this season I guarantee you, those unexpected bills that will come in the Winter season - God will see to it that they are paid. Those things that will be bitter and cold - God will bring peace and comfort. God does not change because of our circumstances - He is sending His Word to change our circumstances. Store Up.

People's Choice Services, LLC

Charlene Outterbridge, Agent

6218 Chew Avenue
Philadelphia, PA 19138
Business Number: (215)843-6001
Fax Number: (267)285-0163
peopleschoicellc@gmail.com

AUTO ● HOME ● LIFE ● HEALTH ● INSURANCE ● NOTARY
● INSTANT TAGS & REGISTRATION

"Where People Come First"

> Tell me how am I supposed to live without you, now that I've been loving you for so long? Mom, tell me how I'm supposed to live without you - and how am I supposed to carry on, when all that I'm living for is going (gone).....

The Love and Her Lover

By Jennifer Marlowe

I'm sitting on my mother's bed - hand in hand, smiling at her and that's the song that came to my mind. Tears welled up in my eyes, I turn my head away and did my silent cry that I've become accustom to. These days I've become a professional with much practice. My introduction to the sweetest love was by a natural gesture of embrace and worship. Meet my first consistent love, "My Mom", who introduced me to the greatest lover of all, "Jesus Christ". As a child, my mother would hold me tight and close and rock me gently in her arms, singing Jesus loves the little children. It was through my mom that I undoubtedly knew that, Yes! Jesus loved me.

This is the same lover who I have watched my mom get closer to during her sickness. With whispers of worship from her lips and her hands raised to the heavens, I listen in as she conducts her secret reverence and silent conversations with Jesus. Though my heart was taught to love, He became the lover who I was now angry with. Allow me to be candid - He was the lover I knew as a healer beyond the shadow of a doubt, yet my mom is living through her final days given by the doctor in pain. So why hasn't God healed her?

His words are above His name and His promises are sure because he has proven Himself to me as a way-maker. I've stood on His promises when I was in the midst of my trial. He became my lawyer in the courtroom. I remember standing on His word and having faith that He will do just what He said. The scripture states, "Without faith it is impossible to please God." (Hebrews 11:6). So to please my lover, all I had to do was believe in Him and then He'd give me the desire of my heart. TO BE FREE from court charges was my spiritual and literal desire - but that's another story. That is just one example of HIS proven grace.

Now I am believing for my mother's healing (Isaiah 54:4). He has given His promise that by His stripes we are healed and I'm waiting for it to be manifested.

> "Didn't come here to cry, didn't come to break down, it seems my dreams are coming to an end...."

I'm believing, I'm trusting, I'm having faith, I'm waiting, I'm … IAM…It's during my daily routine at 7pm - getting in my mom's bed and laying with her that I'm overcome and consumed by the peace my mom possesses. It is as if she is saying, I trust you Lord, let your will be done, I'm in your hands. This is what gives me strength for her - but a part of me feels selfish, in that I want my mommie to be here with me. I've known this woman all my life - she's loved me world without end and without any reservations. I can't fathom living life without her. She had been my physical savior - how am I going to live without her? Then I hear the words of my lover, "You can do all things through Me because I have given you the strength."

The lyrics continue to play in my head. Without missing a beat - and as if we were listening to that same melodic message, I felt my mom's hands rubbing my legs. My silent crying comes into play; my sobs are muffled by my sighs to seek strength, my eyes drained from its tears. I thought to myself, what's my dream? My dream is for my mom to see me my sister and my daughter happily married - and

possibly meet my grandchild (LOL) her great-grand, but will she be here? I ask my other lover (who knows everything Jesus Christ), will my dreams come into fruition? Then He said," Trust in me with all thine heart and lean not to thine own understanding." Feeling the comfort of His word, I wrapped myself in His presence - then my mom whispered in my ear, "I'll never leave you or forsake you and Baby Girl", she loved me and all things worked good for the purpose I called her for. Then the tears start flowing and I'm bawling because I heard my mom saying in her frail voice, "Devil you think you got me but all things work together for my good, I'm going home to heaven ...

Now I can let go of my love, MY MOM to go home to our lover CHRIST JESUS!!

A Dedication to my Mother Myrtle Cox

PURPOSEFUL WAIT MINISTRY

PRESENTS

"Waiting on His Purpose"

Join us for an Anointed, Prophetic move of God as we worship the Lord for His timing in our lives!

Host
Rebecca Rush

Guest Speaker

Minister Cala Allison
Move Of God Ministries
Collingdale PA

"He has made everything beautiful in its time. He has also set eternity in the hearts of men; yet they cannot fathom what God has done from beginning to the end." Ecclesiastes 3:11

Praise Dancers "Peculiar Prayz"

Psalmist Dovita Francis

Friday, December 13th at 7pm
Brand New Life Christian Center
6301 Germantown Avenue.
Philadelphia, PA 19144

For more information contact
Rebecca Rush
267-540-3136

Prophetess Kelly Crews

Exclusive Interview By Joanna Birchett

Gospel4U: Welcome Prophetess Kelly Crews! Thank you very much for taking the time by giving Gospel 4 U Magazine the opportunity to share more about what God has been doing in your life. Amen!

Kelly Crews: Amen...Thank You!

G4U: I want you to go ahead Prophetess Kelly and tell us about who Kelly Crews is.

KC: …Well first let me say thank you for the opportunity to be featured in Gospel 4 U Magazine, Kelly Crews is a down to earth person who loves The Lord and honestly speaking outside of my title I am a loving, creative person. I believe God has equipped me with so much for right now in my life. I'm so excited about what he's doing… I'm a mother…author, all kinds of stuff. First in for most I always like to say I'm a touchable down to earth person because I never want to be like "Oh Kelly Crews…" You know… I just want to be what God has called me to be.

G4U: Amen! That is awesome! That's awesome! How long have you been in ministry?

KC: I've grown up in the church because my father was a Pastor. As far as my ministry …My Ministry has been in existence for 10 years, actually now, because it dispersed in 2003 but… I've grown up in the church, I've always been involved in Ministry, but officially I got saved in 1993…

G4U: Wow that is awesome! Ha-ha ... Well I read your bio and see you have two wonderful children tell us about them.

KC: My children are amazing... My son is 20 years old and a junior in college…

G4U: Wow…You don't look like you have a 20 year old….Ha-ha

KC: Ha-ha… Thank God!

G4U: Amen!

KC: My daughter is 15 … she is a sophomore in High school… Right now this week I have some downtime... I do have a grand baby, my son has a son he's going to be two November 1st… He is actually sleeping on one of the chairs right now…

G4U: Aww…

KC: I just enjoy keeping him when I can… My kids are awesome… They are good kids and I'm just looking forward to seeing what God is going to do in their lives.

G4U: Amen! I relate, I'm a mother myself … Having kids and being in such high demand cannot be easy, God sends you from State to State…How do you think they deal with that?

KC: They are very supportive they travel with me… My son actually just came to Baltimore with me and my daughter went with me to New Jersey near Philadelphia with me… So yeah they travel a lot with me as they can... and I thank God that they are very understanding… I also make sure that I can make quality time for them, because that is very important, right now my grandson birthday party is in two weeks so I keep that date open… I make sure that important things with my family is taken care of and I make sure I support them in every way…

G4U: Wow … I take my hat off to you that is a blessing to hear, because a lot of times people go in ministry and somewhere down the line they tend to forget the children, but that is a blessing that they are able to travel with you… That is such a blessing. I see you have the grace of the prophetic. I say the grace because I know it takes the grace of God for anyone to handle any ministry that have been placed in their hands … talk to us about the gift of prophecy…

KC: …Well it's something I believe …It's an amazing gift and I'm just honored… I'm humbled and honored that God would use me to be his mouthpiece… It's been amazing how God can do so many things through the gift of prophecy, walking in the Grace of that gift allows me to speak into people lives and it's amazing an thing and a amazing place to be. But I love what God is doing.

G4U: I totally agree Woman of God, in these times everyone wants to be a Prophet and that is a good thing to desire, but do you think training is required?

KC: Yes most definately. At my church, we are doing a class on Saturday mornings, its called Perfective Provision. I think people need to be trained a little better in any office that they are called to be in, so that they are able to function by the Spirit and just being able to understand the true function of it. Relationship with God is key and no one can make themselves a Prophet, that is a God ordained gift.

G4U: Wow! So Tell me Kelly are you married, single or divorced?

To read more of the interview with Prophetess Kelly Crews, please go to http://issuu.com/home/publications and read our digital magazine
December 1, 2013

Finishing Strong

"Your words have been harsh against Me," Says the LORD, "Yet you say, 'What have we spoken against You?' You have said, 'It is useless to serve God; What profit is it that we have kept His ordinance, And that we have walked as mourners before the LORD of hosts? So now we call the proud blessed, For those who do wickedness are raised up; They even tempt God and go free.'" (Malachi 3:13-15, NKJV)

Amina Maybank

As we see in Malachi chapter 3, the people of God were weary in serving Him. They were weary in their commitment to God. They were delivered and serving God, but they were still suffering. Their time of prosperity that God promised had not yet come. Because of that, they began to have the wrong perspective and their hearts were far from God. They believed the unbeliever was prospering and the people of God were suffering. This sounds like the people of God today. When we serve God, minister to others, and live uprightly before the Lord, but our time of prosperity doesn't come when we think it should come, we can speak harshly of God even in our hearts.

We in the Body of Christ need to push. Push until whatever God has put in us is birthed. Push our way to the house of God. Push in our prayer lives. Push ourselves in serving God from our hearts, not our needs. God needs people that will push to the finish line. How can we quit and give up on God? The One who delivered us. The One who saved us. The One who keeps us. He is God. God is not a man, that he should lie; neither the son of man, that he should repent: hath he said, and shall he not do it? Or hath he spoken, and shall he not make it good? (Numbers 23:19)

To contact Amina Maybank for any ministry details please email her at wordsfromheaven2012@yahoo.com and check out her blogpage at www.aminaswords.blogspot.com

We must have faith in God to finish the race that is set before us. God is a faithful God. If we have His Spirit in us, we need to be faithful people in return. When you meet your Heavenly Father on that Day, may the Lord say to you, 'Well done, good and faithful servant; you have been faithful over a few things, I will make you ruler over many things. Enter into the joy of your Lord.'

Finish Strong.

"WHOM THE SON SETS FREE IS FREE INDEED"

If you would have told me that I would be restored today and free from the wiles of the enemy, I would blatantly disagree with you. As Paul states in Philippians 4:12..." I have learned the secret of being content in any and every situation..." For me that was a defining moment because for many years I was content on fulfilling a predestinated walk of despair. I lived in my own personal prison that operated between my ears; my mind. At an early age I experience emotional and mental abuse that set the stage for depression which led to a life centered on drugs and alcohol. Secretly, I lived a life of homosexuality and was embarrassed, ashamed, and often felt like an outcast from society. I pursued this passion of drinking and drugging like it was the prerequisite to pass exams that would ordinarily allow me to reach my pinnacle which was my impeding death. I died often in this pursuit where I sold my soul to the devil for worldly possessions and the chance for love in all the wrong places. It took me from state to state seeking a deliverer who I found in men and women who were my equals in  the arena of darkness. I often heard the statement of what is a nice girl like you doing in a place like this, the pictures that were painted by my stepmother was that I was not a nice girl, and I would never amount to anything. If you tell a child everyday that she is nothing, well that child will believe that and the blueprint for that life is set.

I soon began a journey of proving to my stepmother how right she was, so I went about fulfilling her every dream of being nothing. As a little girl who was the billboard to be molested by relatives' alcohol and drugs became a welcomed distraction. I no longer had to think about the disgusting feelings of lying on a basement floor knowing that my mother was upstairs aware of the abuse. I later found myself waking up in bed with different men and women leaving me feeling even dirtier, but I would wash it away with another drink. I had sexual relations with husbands and wives with some being supposedly Christians. I had crossed that invisible line to hell and just knew that there was no turning back. Suicide became a daily thought; I tried to kill myself on occasions. I had fallen down the totem pole so low that it was no point in trying to return.

My oldest brother was killed in October of 1986, I will never forget receiving the call in my aunts New York apartment. My reason for moving to I was on a binge for a year and if I could not sink any lower I caught a glimpse of myself in the mirror downing a bottle of rubbing alcohol because I had no money. I did what I would normally do is convince myself that it didn't happen.

I had mastered lying to myself and convincing myself that my lies were truths. I could no longer distinguish the true from the false. I believed that nobody knew what I was doing when actually everyone knew but me. I thought since I didn't have the courage to kill myself then jail would be the next best thing for me. At least I would get three "hots and a cot" as they would say on the street. I thought I was done, unemployable, high school dropout, lesbian, alcoholic and an addict. The voice that I know now to be the Holy Spirit imparted in me go get help for people with drinking problems. I never heard that before and I went to rehab. I thank God for sending me there first because if I would have gone to church it would not have helped me. Many churches today focus on the inside, complain about the outside, but do not know how to help people like myself and unknowingly chase them back to the outside. AA taught me how to stay sober and once I learned how to do that God sent Sister Gwendolyn Cook to minister to me about Jesus. I attended a large church, received my salvation but sat there for eight years tormented because of my past.

Many are sitting in churches today with secrets and afraid to talk to leadership. I felt I could not talk to leadership for being judged so I just went through the motions. I eventually left that church and is now a member of a church that cares about people and not just statistics. I have established a wonderful relationship with my heavenly Father. Today I have an Associate, Bachelors and soon a Master's in March 2014. I'm a member of both National and International Honor Societies. I have not touched a drink or drug in over (26) years. I've been delivered from depression, homosexuality and currently is the President of "It's Not about Me Ministries." I have been restored "So whom the Son sets free, is free indeed." John 8:36.

SISTER ELLA BESS

Visit my website: itsnotaboutmeministries.org
Email: itsnotaboutmeministry@mail.com

www.HairWithMonica.com

Get the gorgeous **hair** you've always wanted — **for less!**

HairWithMonica.com

610-705-9690

Hair Weaves • Hair Extensions • Lace Wigs

100% Human Hair $47.50

CALL TODAY: 610-705-9690

We have Peruvian, Brazilian, Indian, Malaysian, Cambodian, European, Russian & Mongolian Hair!

A Couple's Meditation: Don't Let Sin Be Your Boss!

Psalm 19:1-14

Just as a masterful work of art displays the exceptional skills, talents and abilities of the artist, so does the awesomeness of God's creation show that He is God. In Psalm 19, David declares that God is the Almighty One who majestically placed the sun, moon, and stars as ornaments in the sky, He set "a tent for the sun," and He continues to ensure that there is nothing "hidden from its (the sun's) heat." Through the ages, all humans, whether sinner or saint, have enjoyed and reaped benefits from God's omnipotent and omniscient creativity. As one who is enthralled by the magnificence of God's Word and work, the Psalmist rightly concludes that mankind should know and reverence God above all others.

In his deference, honor and fear of God, the psalmist prays for an obedient spirit in order to please the Sovereign God who is Master over all. Specifically in verse 13, he asks God to keep him from "presumptuous" or intentional sins, those offenses committed purposefully by one who knows that the act is wrong before God. This is relevant to the married couple because too many times we excuse intentional sins by saying, "that's the way I did it when I was growing up," or we might condone our unpleasant temperament by declaring, "that's just who I am." I've heard husbands and wives tell one another: "You knew I was that way when you married me, so I'm not changing now." We even become arrogant enough to justify our actions by simply stating, "That's the way I felt at the time," thereby exalting ourselves and our feelings over the way God would have us respond. The truth is that there are habits, practices, beliefs, thoughts, etc. in all of our lives that are odious to God and harmful to our marriage relationship, yet we insist on holding on to them.

What sinful way do you continually accommodate and for which you even expect your spouse and God to make room? Today is the day and this is the hour to place our arrogance and the related sins at the feet of Jesus. Like the psalmist, we should ask God to keep us from willful sins and pray that sin not have dominion in our lives. That means we must commit to earnestly seeking God's strength and make the personal choice to surrender the intentional and unintentional wrongs to the One who can tear down strongholds, correct faulty thinking, break sinful habits and renew our troubled minds. It is in God's strength that the Christian couple can gain victory over the powerful, but not invincible, influences that come from our flesh, the devil and the world.

The Spirit of God leads the yielded husband and wife to be the transformed partners who live according to the Sovereign Master's design. Know that Almighty God can and does have the authority and power to change our lives, but first we must make the decision to acknowledge and reject the sins that occupy places of authority. Most of us are married to old sinful ways and bad habits, and it is high time to divorce them on the grounds of irreconcilable differences between the Holy Spirit who dwells in us and the sin that so easily besets us.

Reverend Evelyn Barnes

Though 'divorce' is an unlikely word to be used in a couple's meditation, it is fitting simply because a divorce suggests a transformation and permanent estrangement. Rest assured that a life which is estranged from sin, by the power of the Holy Spirit, is a life that enjoys healthy and satisfying relationships with God and spouse.

THOUGHTS TO PONDER

1. Take responsibility for your wrong actions that are impacting your marriage. Note: Each should articulate his/her sins and not those of the other. This is a "self-inventory."

2. Take steps regarding the sins about which you were convicted: (a) Confess your sins to God and your spouse. (b) Express Godly sorrow as you pray for God's forgiveness and restoration. (c) Ask God for wisdom, strength and courage as you turn away from the old habits that offend Him and are harmful to your marriage. (d) Each day choose to live obediently to the will and way of God.

Memorable thought:

As image bearers of the Most High God, we have the ability to make choices. Today, seize the opportunity to love God more meaningfully by choosing to obey Him and separate from the sins that interfere with your relationship with Him and your spouse.

Rev. Evelyn Barnes has been married for 42 years to Pastor Hubert Barnes of the Star of Hope Baptist Church, located @ 7137 Hegermen St., Philadelphia, Pa.19135. Email: ecwbarnes@aol.com

Hours of Operation

Monday Thru Friday from 6:00 AM to 5:30 PM.

For ages Infancy to 13 years old.

Take the first step by registering your child.

LIMITED SPACE AVAILABLE

* Open House Tours Daily *

CHRISTIAN YOUTH MINISTRIES

A SAFE AND FRIENDLY ENVIRONMENT

450 E North Street
Carlisle, PA 17013
Phone: (717) 241-4296
Fax: (717) 241-4413
Email: cymdcc2008@yahoo.com
Web: www.cymdcc.com

STATE LICENSED

By the Department of Welfare

Juan Rivera (Owner and Operator)
Shirley Hinton (Operations Director)

Great is your mercy towards me

The Book of Genesis gave us the account of the great sin of high treason committed by Adam the federal head of humanity when he willfully disobeyed God. Because of one man's disobedience many were made sinners. (Rom 5:12) Wherefore, as by one man sin entered the world and death by sin and so death passed upon all men. For that all have sinned because all were in Adam. Because of Adam's transgression, all were born in sin and sin separated us from fellowship with our creator. Even in Adam's transgression, we can see the mercy of God by removing him from the garden not allowing him to live eternally in that fallen state. God who is rich in mercy desired fellowship with men. Mercy is an act of God, his compassion towards us. No one but Jesus ever qualified to bring God and man together. He was fully God and fully man. Christ is our propitiation – our mercy seat.

In exodus 25, the ark emphasized the person and the mercy seat emphasized the purposed of Christ, nothing but deity could offer saving grace. In the entire universe there was no moral sinless blood to be found except that of the sinless Lamb of God. The mercy seat is where God met with Moses. The mercy seat typifies Christ where the mercy and truth are met together; righteousness and peace have kissed each other (Ps. 85:10).

Under the law, mercy and truth could not meet. Righteousness and peace could not kiss or greet each other. However, in Christ, the two will meet. Peace and reconciliation are obtainable only through Christ, typified by the blood – sprinkled mercy seat. Christ our mercy seat is a place of rest, Jesus calls entreatingly – come unto me all ye that labor and are heavy laden and I will give you rest. Take my yoke upon you and learn of me, for I am meek and lowly in heart and ye shall find rest for your souls (Matt 11:28-29). In Christ, God rests His lawful case against us, wherein He hath made us accepted in the beloved (Eph 1:6). There is no need for sin consciousness–we are accepted in the beloved. The book of Hebrew's tells us that Christ, our sympathetic High Priest, ascended and passed through the heavens. He can be touched with our weaknesses, infirmities and liabilities to the assault of temptation, for he was tempted in every respect as we are, but did not sin. Let us (every believer) fearlessly, confidently and boldly draw near (not away) to the Throne of Grace (the throne of God's unmerited favor) that we may receive mercy for our failures and mess-ups and find grace to help us, for every need – our need of peace; our need of strength; our need of endurance; our need of faith; our need of love; our need of forgiveness; and our need of stability coming just when we need it. God's eternal mercy is wide enough and long enough to cover everyone who abides in Christ.

Apostle Sandra Hayden

PRAYER

by Cynthia B. Jackson

1 Thessalonians 5:17 says, pray without ceasing (NKJV). Prayer moves mountains; Prayer moves people; and Prayer moves heaven.

Prayer is the most powerful thing we can do, yet it seems to be the hardest thing for the people of God to master and become proficient in. Jesus gave us instructions on how to pray (Matthew 6:9-13). He has ordained us and called us to pray His word over our lives so that His will can be manifested.

Prayer moves mountains. When we are faced with situations that seem like mountains, we are to use the Word of God in prayer, to move them. God told Ezekiel in chapter 21:2 to drop the word toward the holy places and prophesy…. If God instructed Ezekiel to drop the word, surely we can drop His Word on the mountains standing in the way of His purpose being fulfilled.

Prayer moves people. God has called us to pray for one another. You will never know how your prayers changed the course of a person's life. In Acts chapter 4:31 the people of God prayed; the earth shook, they were filled with the Holy Spirit and spoke the word of God in boldness. This is what prayer does. It moves you and others into another dimension in the realm of the spirit to become whole and powerful.

Prayer moves heaven. God is listening to our prayers. Not only is He listening, but he is assigning angles to move on our behalf. Psalm 91:11 says, *He has given His angels charge over us to keep us in all our ways (NKJV)*. God is moving heaven at the hearing of our prayers. Don't stop declaring God's word over your life and the lives of others. God is faithful - change is on the way.

Author Dennean Handfield's NEW Novel!!!
Journey to wholeness

A fiction novel Journey to wholeness targeted towards teenage girls. For additional information please visit www.denneanhandfield.com

Info@DenneanHandField.com - (610) 400-5288

DenneanHandfield
www.DenneanHandfield.com

"Patrice Johnson Is a teenage girl who struggles with loving herself. She is in a relationship with the star basketball player and hears rumors of cheating. As Patrice battles the decision of leaving her boyfriend she also has to maintain good grades for college acceptance. If you are a teenage girl who isn't aware of your true value than this book is for you. Join Patrice on her journey to wholeness."

— Deneen Handfield

Do I Have a Purpose

Victoria Tindal

Many feel that if God didn't call you to be a pastor, evangelist, prophet or sing on the choir that we weren't called at all. We feel like we just got thrown into the "general" category and aren't special in any way. Then that causes us to kind of stray away from God. It's like everybody else has something so specific and unique that God called them to do except for you. But as we can see in all of creation, God never just throws anything together. Everything is intricately made with a purpose and for a purpose! Why would you be any different? Don't you know that you are your ministry! Ministry isn't confined to a church. The word ministry actually means to serve.

What God gave you is a way you can serve ,because that's what ministry is all about!

1 Corinthians 4:1-2

"This is how one should regard us, as stewards of the mysteries of God. Moreover, it is required of stewards that they be found faithful"

There are so many ways to serve God and so much He can do with who He made you! But you have to be faithful. When God tells you to do something and gives you a great way to use your gifts to serve, what are you doing with it? Are you letting the idea sit around and get stale? Are you putting it on the back burner or half doing it? Don't miss out because you cant be faithful with what He gave you and then look at other peoples ministries and get all down when you see the fruit of their faithfulness.

God is our source. When you give Him your whole heart and build your relationship with Him trust that He will show your purpose and your calling.

Take the limits off of God! He can use your talents and passions to advance His Kingdom!

Victoria Tindal is a Minister at Empowerment LifeChanging Worship Center Millville, NJ under Pastor Lawrence & Prophetess Ayanna Moore. Connect with Victoria at
www.christoverdrive.com

www.ingramcontent.com/pod-product-compliance
Lightning Source LLC
Chambersburg PA
CBHW041227040426

42444CB00002B/78